Be a Person
After God's
Own Heart

A Chronological Journal Bible Study of
David and the Psalms

Sandy K Cook

with contributions from Darlene Hann

Published by Psalm 30 Publishing,
© 2019 Sandra K. Cook, All rights reserved.

Cover Photo credit: Jerusalem Tower of David, Wikimedia.org commons, public domain image.

ISBN-13: 978-1-948953-02-3

Psalm 30 Publishing
P.O. Box 491328,
Lawrenceville, GA 30049

Unless otherwise noted, Bible verses printed in this book are taken from translations of the Bible that are in the Public Domain. Verses have been taken from an ASV-based, Public Domain translation, and have been modified to revert back from the use of the formal name of God, which was added in that translation. Within this book, God is addressed as God, The Lord, or Jesus throughout the book. As required by the Public Domain permissions of the secondary Public Domain source, the specific secondary Public Domain source will remain unidentified in this publication, because some verses have been modified and no longer directly reflect the content of the specific public domain source.

DEDICATION

This book is dedicated to my church family at the Bridge Church Atlanta, especially to our Sisterhood on Wednesday Mornings, without which I would not have been encouraged to dive into developing this Bible Study.

ACKNOWLEDGMENTS

My heartfelt thanks and appreciation is for Darlene Hann. She faithfully read through this entire study as I was designing it. Darlene submitted her thoughtful reflection questions for each day's reading. She helped insure this study contains the best possible reflection questions by helping expand the pool of questions from which I could choose for each day's reading. I'd also like to thank the women of the Sisterhood at the Bridge Church Atlanta for their help in finding my typing errors and for their encouragement about the quality of this study.

HOW THIS JOURNAL BIBLE STUDY WORKS

This is an inductive Bible study in journal format. For each reading, there is a full page for your personal notes. You can use the journal space to write down any thoughts, insights, or questions you have, or to draw the visions that come to your mind.

After your journal reading, there is a section with reflection and life application questions. Some of the questions will relate directly to David or the events in the reading. Others are application questions for you to reflect on how these Bible verses might apply to your life.

Your answers can be as brief or as deep as you would like to make them. However, you will get more out of the study if you pray and meditate on the scripture and questions before you write down your answers.

This study is laid out in chronological order for David's life. Some of the Psalms are out of order, based on when they are believed to have been written. That is because David sometimes wrote his Psalms at times other than when the actual events occurred. It is also unknown when some of the Psalms were written, so liberties were taken in placing the Psalms, usually with chronological events that seem to match the focus of the Psalm.

As a preliminary question for this study, ask yourself, "What does it mean to you to be a person after God's own heart?" Read Psalm 16:8, Joshua 22:5, and 2 Chronicles 16:9 to help form your ideas about having a heart after God's own heart.

Pray for your understanding about this defining characteristic of David and how the Lord might help you make it a characteristic that describes you. Picture what it might mean if people said you were a person after God's own heart at the end of your life.

What does it mean to you to have a heart after God's own heart?

_____

_____

_____

_____

_____

_____

_____

_____

_____

_____

_____

✓	Reading	History	Psalms	Subject
	1	1 Samuel 16	Psalms 8 & 23	David anointed
	2	1 Samuel 17	Psalms 9 & 25	David versus Goliath
	3	1 Samuel 18	Psalms 26 & 27	David and Saul
	4	1 Samuel 19	Psalms 11 & 59	Saul hates David
	5	1 Samuel 20	Psalms 1 & 7	David & Jonathan
	6	1 Samuel 21	Psalms 34 & 56	David takes bread
	7	1 Samuel 22	Psalms 35 & 52	David flees from Saul
	8	1 Samuel 23	Psalms 31 & 54	David is pursued
	9	1 Samuel 24	Psalms 57 & 58	David spares Saul
	10	1 Samuel 25	Psalms 36 & 128	David and Abigail
	11	1 Samuel 26	Psalms 17 & 64	David spares Saul again
	12	1 Samuel 27 – 1 Samuel 28:2	Psalms 61 & 141	David dwells with the Philistines
	13	1 Samuel 29	Psalms 121 &130	Philistines mistrust David
	14	1 Samuel 30	Psalms 124 & 140	David defeats the Amalekites
	15	1 Samuel 31	Psalms 40 & 63	Saul and sons slain
	16	2 Samuel 1	Psalms 16 & 19	David mourns Jonathan and Saul
	17	2 Samuel 2	Psalms 94 & 125	David anointed king of Judah and battles Israel
	18	2 Samuel 3	Psalms 14 & 86	David is King and Abner is murdered by Joab
	19	2 Samuel 4	Psalms 10 & 142	Ish-bosheth is killed & his death is avenged
	20	2 Samuel 5	Psalms 107 & 108	David conquers the Philistines
	21	1 Chronicles 11	Psalms 133 & 138	David anointed King of Israel
	22	1 Chronicles 13 & 2 Samuel 6	Psalms 15 & 139	Ark is brought to Israel; Uzzah struck down
	23	1 Chronicles 15	Psalms 68 & 132	David brings the Ark into Jerusalem
	24	Psalm 68	Psalms 105 & 106	David writes about bringing the Ark to Jerusalem

✓	Reading	History	Psalms	Subject
	25	1 Chronicles 16	Psalms 24 & 96	Ark Placed in a Tent and David Worships
	26	2 Samuel 7	Psalms 2 & 33	The Lord makes a covenant with David
	27	Psalm 89	Psalms 110 & 111	The Lord's covenant with David
	28	2 Samuel 9	Psalms 101 & 122	David brings Mephibosheth into his family
	29	1 Chronicles 18	Psalms 22 & 60	David's victories
	30	2 Samuel 10	Psalms 20 & 21	Ammonites versus David
	31	2 Samuel 11	Psalms 38 & 53	David desires Bathsheba and kills Uriah
	32	2 Samuel 12	Psalms 32 & 51	David warned and his child dies; Solomon born
	33	2 Samuel 13	Psalms 13 & 28	Ammon, Tamar and Absalom
	34	2 Samuel 14	Psalms 4 & 12	David lets Absalom return
	35	2 Samuel 15	Psalms 3, 70 & 71	David flees Absalom
	36	2 Samuel 16	Psalms 69 &109	David, Absalom, and Ahithophel
	37	2 Samuel 17	Psalms 55 & 62	David is saved by Hushai
	38	2 Samuel 18	Psalms 143 & 144	Absalom is killed
	39	2 Samuel 19	Psalms 39 & 41	David returns to Jerusalem
	40	2 Samuel 20 & 21	Psalms 5 & 29	War with Philistines
	41	2 Samuel 22	Psalms 18 & 100	David's song of deliverance
	42	2 Samuel 23	Psalms 91 & 95	The last words of David
	43	1 Chronicles 21	Psalms 6 & 30	Census brings judgment & David builds an altar
	44	1 Chronicles 22-23:1	Psalms 118 & 131	David prepares building supplies for the temple
	45	1 Kings 1	Psalms 37 & 72	David's old age; Solomon Anointed King
	46	1 Chronicles 28	Psalms 112 & 115	David's Charges to Israel and Solomon
	47	1 Chronicles 29	Psalms 103 & 145	David's gifts to the temple, his prayers & death
	48	1 Kings 2	Psalms 65, 116, 127	David instructs Solomon and David's Death

READING 1 ~ 1 SAMUEL 16

READING 1 ~ PSALMS 8 & 23

READING 1 ~ QUESTIONS

1) What do you think the Lord is looking for when he examines our hearts? Explain.

_____

_____

_____

_____

_____

_____

_____

2) What strengths will God find when he examines your heart?

_____

_____

_____

_____

_____

_____

_____

3) What weaknesses or sins will God find when he examines your heart?

_____

_____

_____

_____

_____

_____

_____

4) In what ways can you grow and change, so that God will see a person after His own heart in you?

_____

_____

_____

_____

_____

_____

_____

READING 1 ~ QUESTIONS

5) What insights or questions occur to you when you read in 1 Sam. 16:14 that Saul was tormented by an evil spirit "from God"?

_____

_____

_____

_____

_____

_____

_____

6) What are some reasons that God may allow an evil spirit to come upon a person?

_____

_____

_____

_____

_____

_____

_____

7) In what ways does the Lord restore your soul?

_____

_____

_____

_____

_____

_____

_____

8) What insights or thoughts of comfort occur to you as you take a fresh look at Psalm 23?

_____

_____

_____

_____

_____

_____

_____

READING 2 ~ 1 SAMUEL 17

READING 2 ~ PSALMS 9 & 25

READING 2 ~ QUESTIONS

1)   Ask the Holy Spirit to reveal to you the "giants" you have allowed to taunt and harass you in your life. How can you respond differently to your situation(s), as you reflect on David's response to Goliath?

_____

_____

_____

_____

_____

_____

_____

2)   Read the interaction between Eliab and David carefully. What insights occur to you when you consider how your children are permitted or required to talk to and treat their siblings?

_____

_____

_____

_____

_____

_____

_____

3) What were all of the men of Israel focusing on which made them afraid of Goliath?

_____

_____

_____

_____

_____

_____

4) What was David focusing on which allowed him to be unafraid of Goliath?

_____

_____

_____

_____

_____

_____

5) When you think of the enemy of your soul, what phrases or verses from Psalm 9 give you encouragement?

_____

_____

_____

_____

_____

_____

_____

6) It is said of Psalm 25 that you can see the heart of the man after God's Own Heart within it. Where do you see David's heart is after God's Own Heart in this psalm and in his battle against Goliath?

_____

_____

_____

_____

_____

_____

7) What do you read in David's words in Psalm 25:1-2a & 25:4-5a about his attitude toward God that you have already recognized by reading previously of David's actions? How important do you think this attitude might be for you in seeking after God's heart?

_____

_____

_____

_____

_____

_____

8) Pray Psalm 25 out loud, expressing your true feelings. What aspects of this Psalm speak most deeply to your heart? Turn those into a prayer and write it down.

_____

_____

_____

_____

_____

READING 3 ~ 1 SAMUEL 18

READING 3 ~ PSALMS 26 & 27

READING 3 ~ QUESTIONS

1) What attitudes or actions of Saul in in 1 Samuel 18 are likely to have caused the Lord to depart from him? (1 Sam 18:12)

_____

_____

_____

_____

_____

_____

2) In 1 Samuel 18:14 we read that in everything he did, David had success. Based on what you know of David's life to this point, how does David's "success" differ from our culture's definition of success?

_____

_____

_____

_____

_____

_____

_____

3) Do people who have the Lord with them always prosper in all of their ways? What examples can you provide? (1 Sam 18:14)

_____

_____

_____

_____

_____

4) What really made Saul into David's enemy continually? 1 Sam. 18:29

_____

_____

_____

_____

_____

_____

READING 3 ~ QUESTIONS

5) What does David wish to do for the Lord in Psalm 26? What do you wish to do for the Lord?

_____

_____

_____

_____

_____

_____

6) What does it look like to walk in integrity? (Ps 26)

_____

_____

_____

_____

_____

_____

7) According to Psalm 27, what is the one thing that David has asked from the Lord? What is one thing you would ask of the Lord? Ask it.

_____

_____

_____

_____

_____

_____

8) What "examples to follow" do you find in reading David's words in Psalm 27?

_____

_____

_____

_____

_____

_____

READING 4 ~ 1 SAMUEL 19

READING 4 ~ PSALMS 11 & 59

READING 4 ~ QUESTIONS

1) Other than having the evil spirit on Saul, why did Saul have such a deep hatred for David?

_____

_____

_____

_____

_____

_____

2) What character attributes of Saul are working against his own success?

_____

_____

_____

_____

_____

_____

3) If the spirit of God came upon you and you began prophesying, what type of changes would you expect to take place in your life and thinking toward God? In what way?

_____

_____

_____

_____

_____

_____

4) What seems to be David's heartfelt attitude as he begins a transient life, fleeing from Saul, even though David has been anointed by God to become king?

_____

_____

_____

_____

_____

_____

READING 4 ~ QUESTIONS

6)   Have you ever had a friend like Jonathan? What did that person's friendship mean to you?

_____
_____
_____
_____
_____
_____

7)   What character traits do you see in Jonathan that you want the Holy Spirit to develop in you? Ask God for these traits.

_____
_____
_____
_____
_____
_____

8)   How does a righteous person take refuge in the Lord? (Ps 11)

_____
_____
_____
_____
_____
_____

9)   From David's words in Psalms 11 and 59, what would be a good way to respond when all seems against you? How would you demonstrate being a person after God's Own Heart?

_____
_____
_____
_____
_____
_____

READING 5 ~ 1 SAMUEL 20

READING 5 ~ QUESTIONS

1) In 1 Samuel 20:13, Jonathan refers to the Lord being with his father, Saul. In what ways is the Lord with Saul?

_____

_____

_____

_____

_____

_____

2) What factors make Jonathan choose to help David live, even though Jonathan would inherit the kingdom if David died? Why wouldn't Jonathan put himself on the throne?

_____

_____

_____

_____

_____

_____

3) How do you suppose the Lord views Jonathan's heart and his actions as they relate to both Saul and David?

_____

_____

_____

_____

_____

4) Why did David weep more than Jonathan? (1 Sam 20:41)

_____

_____

_____

_____

_____

_____

READING 5 ~ QUESTIONS

5) What factors cause Saul to be driven after David with intent to kill David?

_____

_____

_____

_____

_____

_____

6) Read Psalm 1 in several different versions. What truths speak to your heart from this very important psalm? Rewrite those truths in the form of a prayer.

_____

_____

_____

_____

_____

_____

7) What would your life look like if you were a firmly planted tree by streams of water? (Psalm 1)

_____

_____

_____

_____

_____

_____

8) Look for clues in Psalm 7 about the character of God. How does being reminded of what God is like help you to follow David's example of praise and thankfulness (see vs 17) during hard times?

_____

_____

_____

_____

_____

READING 6 ~ 1 SAMUEL 21

READING 6 ~ PSALMS 34 & 56

READING 6 ~ QUESTIONS

1) Does God require scrupulous honesty at all times from His children? (Does He condone, for example, the dishonesty of those who hid the Jews from the Nazis during WWII? What about those who illegally smuggle Bibles into countries where Bibles are not allowed?)

_____
_____
_____
_____
_____
_____
_____

2) Is David's deceptiveness in 1 Samuel 21 a sin? Consider 1 Samuel 16:2. Carefully read Exodus 20:16, which we often take to mean "do not lie". What does it actually say, and how might it apply to David's actions in this chapter?

_____
_____
_____
_____
_____
_____
_____

3) Do you think David was acting out of his own human nature when he misrepresented himself to both Ahimelech and Achish, or could God have been giving David creative ways of handling difficult situations? What are your conclusions as they apply to tricky situations in your own life?

_____
_____
_____
_____
_____
_____

4) How did the Lord deliver David from all of his fears, troubles, and afflictions? (Ps. 34)

_____
_____
_____
_____
_____
_____
_____

5) Read Exodus 12:46 and John 19:33-36. What thoughts and insights occur to you as you recognize Psalm 34:20 as Messianic prophecy?

_____
_____
_____
_____
_____
_____
_____

6) Can you draw any parallels between David's anointing as king and then waiting for so many years to actually become king and the promises we read of Jesus reigning as King of Kings and Lord of Lords, to whom one day every knee shall bow? (Psalm 34)

_____
_____
_____
_____
_____
_____
_____

7) The Psalms in today's readings show David's heart after God, but his actions in 1 Samuel 21 might not demonstrate full faith in God, if David was acting out of his human nature. In what way can you relate David's words versus his actions when it comes to your own words and actions, and having a heart after God?

_____
_____
_____
_____
_____

8) Have you have ever been fearful for your life or personal safety? What role did or would God have in such a situation? (Ps 56)

_____
_____
_____
_____
_____

READING 7 ~ QUESTIONS

1) In 1 Samuel 22:3, we see that David is waiting to take action until he knows what God will do. How does waiting on God demonstrate having a heart after God?

_____
_____
_____
_____
_____
_____
_____

2) Why do you think Doeg, the Edomite, was willing to kill all of the priests and their families when no one else would? What insights can you gain about Doeg's motives from Psalm 52?

_____
_____
_____
_____
_____
_____
_____

3) What makes it difficult for you to wait on God's Direction in your life?

_____
_____
_____
_____
_____
_____

4) In what circumstances are you seeking God's Direction in your life, and how will you know when your wait is over?

_____
_____
_____
_____
_____
_____
_____

READING 7 ~ QUESTIONS

5) In Psalm 35, David asks the Lord, "Say to my soul, 'I am your salvation.'" How does the Lord speak to our souls?

_____

_____

_____

_____

_____

_____

_____

6) List the actions David took when evil came against him, as stated in Psalm 35.

_____

_____

_____

_____

_____

_____

_____

7) In Psalm 35, what is David petitioning for from God? What is David's desired outcome?

_____

_____

_____

_____

_____

_____

8) In the most difficult circumstance you are facing, write a prayer to God stating what you have done so far, and what you would like for the outcome in your situation:

_____

_____

_____

_____

_____

_____

_____

_____

READING 8 ~ 1 SAMUEL 23

READING 8 ~ PSALMS 31 & 54

READING 8 ~ QUESTIONS

1) When making a decision about something of importance, and we inquire of the Lord, what are some ways we can know when we are hearing God's response?

_____
_____
_____
_____
_____
_____
_____

2) Look for attributes of God and His promises in Psalm 31. Write them down.

_____
_____
_____
_____
_____
_____
_____
_____

3) What do you see as "examples to follow" from what David wrote in Psalm 31.

_____
_____
_____
_____
_____
_____
_____

4) In Psalm 31, David is not overly happy with how his life is going so far, yet he praises and expresses his trust in the Lord. When you are conflicted about how your life is going versus knowing that the Lord is present and able to help you, how do you resolve the conflicting emotions in your heart?

_____
_____
_____
_____
_____
_____
_____

READING 8 ~ QUESTIONS

5) In Psalm 31:5, David says he is ransomed by the Lord. In what ways has David been ransomed? If you are a Christian, how have you been ransomed by the Lord?

_____
_____
_____
_____
_____
_____
_____

6) Does God always save his beloved from their enemies? Give some examples of beloved people of God who were not saved from their enemies desire to kill them. (Ps 54)

_____
_____
_____
_____
_____
_____

7) Why do you suppose God lets some of his beloved people perish? Why did God continually protect to David from his enemies? (Ps 54)

_____
_____
_____
_____
_____
_____

8) In what ways will having a heart after God's own heart make you fearless about whatever may come to you in your lifetime? (Ps 54)

_____
_____
_____
_____
_____
_____

READING 9 ~ 1 SAMUEL 24

READING 9 ~ PSALMS 57 & 58

READING 9 ~ QUESTIONS

1) What do you learn about David's heart and character based on his response to his men in 1 Sam. 24:4-7?

_____

_____

_____

_____

_____

_____

_____

2) What principle(s) might we learn from David's refusal to harm "the Lord's anointed"?

_____

_____

_____

_____

_____

_____

_____

_____

3) Have you ever had someone tell you what the Lord was saying to you or about you? How did you or how would you, handle that kind of information? (Example: 1 Sam. 24:4)

_____

_____

_____

_____

_____

_____

_____

4) When someone is hateful toward you or injures you, what steps can you take to effectively wait on the Lord's action, rather than taking any action yourself?

_____

_____

_____

_____

_____

_____

_____

READING 9 ~ QUESTIONS

5) Do you think Saul's change of countenance in this chapter is a true change in his heart toward David? Why or why not?

_____
_____
_____
_____
_____
_____
_____

6) In the Covenant stated in 1 Samuel 24:21, what priorities do Saul's requests reveal within his heart?

_____
_____
_____
_____
_____
_____
_____
_____

7) What things has God accomplished for you in your life? (See Psalm 57:2)

_____
_____
_____
_____
_____
_____
_____

8) Why do some people tend to withhold their true selves from God in their prayers, rather than pour out everything in their hearts to the Lord?

_____
_____
_____
_____
_____
_____
_____

READING 10 ~ QUESTIONS

1) In the beginning of our study, God had Samuel anoint David as king. Now Samuel has died, and David is not yet king. Reflect on the importance of waiting for God's timing and write your thoughts about waiting for God's timing.

_____
_____
_____
_____
_____
_____
_____

2) What ungodly attitudes and actions do we see emerging from David in his response to Nabal in 1 Samuel 25? What similar evil actions and reactions would God warn you about from reading of this?

_____
_____
_____
_____
_____
_____
_____
_____

3) Using Abigail's actions as an example of making up for Nabal's bad behavior, in what ways can you make amends for any of your past bad behavior?

_____
_____
_____
_____
_____
_____

4) What character qualities do you admire in Abigail?

_____
_____
_____
_____
_____
_____

READING 10 ~ QUESTIONS

5) In Psalm 36, what are the contrasting differences between the ungodly and those who know the Lord? (Psalm 36)

_____

_____

_____

_____

_____

_____

_____

6) What happens when the foot of pride or arrogance comes upon Christians? How can we avoid having the foot of pride come upon us?

_____

_____

_____

_____

_____

_____

_____

7) What do you learn about the value of family from Psalm 128? (Realize that "family" can be biological, legal, or spiritual - as in the "family of God".)

_____

_____

_____

_____

_____

8) What does fear of the Lord look like among those who truly fear the lord? Is it a shaking in our shoes, terrified kind of fear or something else? Describe an appropriate fear of the Lord as best you can. (Psalm 128)

_____

_____

_____

_____

_____

READING 11 ~ 1 SAMUEL 26

READING 11 ~ PSALMS 17 & 64

READING 11 ~ QUESTIONS

1) Why do you suppose Saul is again pursuing David in 1 Samuel 26? What do you think truly drives Saul to pursue David?

_____

_____

_____

_____

_____

_____

_____

2) Of what significance would the spear and water jug that David took be to Saul? Why are they important items to demonstrate David's mercy towards Saul?

_____

_____

_____

_____

_____

_____

_____

3) What insights do you gain from the references in 1 Samuel 26, verses 12 and 23, about God's role in this event?

_____

_____

_____

_____

_____

_____

4) What heartfelt feelings towards Saul has David demonstrated in 1 Samuel 24 and 1 Samuel 26?

_____

_____

_____

_____

_____

READING 11 ~ QUESTIONS

5) If the Lord probed your heart and examined you, what types of plans and actions would He find in you toward contentious people in your life? (Ps. 17)

_____
_____
_____
_____
_____
_____
_____
_____
_____

6) Read Psalm 17:14 carefully. Are you ever tempted to focus on this life, as David describes for the wicked? What is David's answer to this tendency (vs 15)

_____
_____
_____
_____
_____
_____
_____
_____
_____

7) In Psalm 64:1, David is issuing his complaint to God. Do you typically complain to God or to other people? Which is preferred or proper and why?

_____
_____
_____
_____
_____
_____
_____

8) In what ways are the inward mind and heart of a man deep, and only seen by God? (Psalm 64)

_____
_____
_____
_____
_____
_____

READING 12 ~ QUESTIONS

1) Why do you suppose that David was welcomed by Achish, king of Gath, as we read in Chapter 27? What motivations would Achish have for allowing David to live in their land?

_____

_____

_____

_____

_____

_____

2) At this point in our reading, where do you think David's true loyalty lies, with the Israelites or is it with the Philistines? What is your reason for thinking as you do?

_____

_____

_____

_____

_____

_____

3) What do you think prompted David's decision to escape to the land of the Philistines - faith, fear, or something else? Why?

_____

_____

_____

_____

_____

_____

_____

4) It appears David and his 600 men made a living by raiding the Geshurites, Girzites and Amalekites--all Canaanites. How do you suppose God viewed this? (Read Lev. 18, Deut. 19:1, Ex. 17:16, and 1 Sam. 15:2 & 18 for insight).

_____

_____

_____

_____

_____

_____

READING 12 ~ QUESTIONS

5) What are some reasons David may have felt compelled to carry out the raids against these enemies of both Israel and the Philistines?

_____

_____

_____

_____

_____

_____

_____

6) What principle from God's instructions to Israel to destroy the nations occupying the Promised Land can you apply to your life when it comes to allowing your enemy or a sin to keep a foothold in your life?

_____

_____

_____

_____

_____

_____

_____

7) In Psalm 61, what does David desire from God? What do you desire as a person with a heart after God?

_____

_____

_____

_____

_____

_____

8) In Psalm 141:6, David says his words are heard because they are pleasant. Find a headline or post that could be offensive to some readers. Write it down, and then rewrite the message to make it more pleasant and easier to receive.

_____

_____

_____

_____

_____

_____

READING 13 ~ PSALMS 121 & 130

READING 13 ~ QUESTIONS

1) Why is David pleasing in Achish's sight and like an angel of God to Achish?

_____

_____

_____

_____

_____

_____

_____

2) Why didn't the Philistine Commanders trust David like Achish did?

_____

_____

_____

_____

_____

_____

_____

3) In what ways is it good for David that the Philistine commanders did not want David and his men to battle with them against the Israelites?

_____

_____

_____

_____

_____

_____

4) Under what circumstances does it feel like the Lord is sleeping rather than making his presence known? (Psalm 121)

_____

_____

_____

_____

_____

_____

_____

5) Why does help from the Lord often look different than we expect it to look? (Psalm 121)

_____
_____
_____
_____
_____
_____
_____
_____

6) When you are in a time of waiting, where will you find hope? Write out any insights the Lord brings to your mind.

_____
_____
_____
_____
_____
_____
_____

7) What should you do when you find yourself "in the depths" of trouble or despair? (Psalm 130)

_____
_____
_____
_____
_____
_____
_____

8) What do you learn about God's heart from Psalm 130:7-8? How can you use this to help you have a heart after God's own heart?

_____
_____
_____
_____
_____
_____

READING 14 ~ QUESTIONS

1) What would your feelings be toward God if you returned home and found everything had been taken and your home was burned? How would your feelings differ if you truly had a heart after God?

_____

_____

_____

_____

_____

2) Why do David's men blame him for the attack on Ziklag? In what ways, if any, would it be David's fault? (Refer to 1 Samuel 29, if needed)

_____

_____

_____

_____

_____

_____

3) How might circumstances been different if David had defied Achish and refused to leave the battle (see Ch. 29)? In what ways might God use ungodly people to affect your circumstances?

_____

_____

_____

_____

_____

_____

4) In verse 6b, we see "David strengthened himself in the Lord his God." What is the significance of David strengthening himself in the Lord in his heart-felt response?

_____

_____

_____

_____

_____

5) How do you strengthen yourself in the Lord?

_____
_____
_____
_____
_____
_____
_____

6) Why is David's distribution of the Amalekite plunder a wise decision? How does this decision demonstrate David's heart after God?

_____
_____
_____
_____
_____
_____
_____
_____
_____

7) Read Psalm 124 in light of the events of 1 Samuel 30. In what ways were David and his men like birds caught in a snare?

_____
_____
_____
_____
_____
_____
_____

8) Which of the evil actions listed in Psalm 140 are present in the world today? What additional evils do you need to pray for protection from?

_____
_____
_____
_____
_____
_____
_____
_____

READING 15 ~ QUESTIONS

1) Why is it fitting and perfect that David was not present at the battle when Jonathan, Saul, and Saul's sons all died?

_____

_____

_____

_____

_____

_____

2) Saul took his sword and fell on it, thereby ending his own life. In what ways does this manner of death reflect the whole of Saul's life?

_____

_____

_____

_____

_____

_____

3) What are your conclusions about the character of Jonathan, after reading about him in 1 Samuel?

_____

_____

_____

_____

_____

_____

4) Is it reasonable to conclude that Jonathan died when and as he did as a result of the sinful life of Saul? Consider 1 Samuel 13:13-14, Exodus 34:7 and James 1:14-15 and write out any thoughts that occur to you.

_____

_____

_____

_____

_____

_____

READING 15 ~ QUESTIONS

5) How might what you learned in the previous question (#4) apply to your life under the New Testament's covenant of grace?

_____
_____
_____
_____
_____
_____
_____
_____

6) If the Lord does not want sacrifices and burnt offerings, what does He want? (Ps 40)

_____
_____
_____
_____
_____
_____
_____
_____

7) When in your life has God set your feet upon a rock, put a new song in your mouth, or shown you great mercy? Write prayer of praise to declare the Lord is your deliverer.

_____
_____
_____
_____
_____
_____
_____

8) In what ways does Psalm 63 reflect everything about David's life to this point, as he looks toward his future?

_____
_____
_____
_____
_____
_____
_____

READING 16 ~ PSALMS 16 & 19

READING 16 ~ QUESTIONS

1) How does the Amalekite's version of Saul's death (2 Sam. 1:6-10) differ from the facts as recorded in 1 Samuel 31? What do you suppose was the Amalekite's motivation?

_____

_____

_____

_____

_____

_____

_____

2) What does David's level of mourning tell us about his true feelings for Saul and Jonathan?

_____

_____

_____

_____

_____

_____

3) Analyze David's Lament over Saul in 2 Samuel 1:19-27. What does David say about Saul that surprises you, if anything?

_____

_____

_____

_____

_____

_____

4) Where is the path of life found, and how does the Lord make it known to you? (Psalm 16:11)

_____

_____

_____

_____

_____

_____

_____

READING 16 ~ QUESTIONS

5) What are some ways you can set the Lord continually before yourself? (Psalm 16:8 and Psalm 19 insights)

_____
_____
_____
_____
_____
_____
_____

6) How is the law of the Lord perfect for restoring and reviving the soul, and why are His judgments more desirable than gold? (Psalm 19)

_____
_____
_____
_____
_____
_____
_____
_____

7) What do you learn about the value of God's word in your life from Psalm 19:7-11?

_____
_____
_____
_____
_____
_____

8) As a person after God's Own Heart, what inspirations for improving your spiritual walk do you receive from Psalm 19?

_____
_____
_____
_____
_____
_____
_____

READING 17 ~ QUESTIONS

1) Do some research to see how many years David waited to become king after he was anointed by Samuel. What can we learn from David's period of waiting when it comes to our calling or our prayers being answered?

_____
_____
_____
_____
_____
_____
_____

2) What characteristics did David demonstrate during his waiting and testing, which reflect favorably on God's selection of David as King?

_____
_____
_____
_____
_____
_____
_____

3) Research and define "the tribes of Israel" in the context of this time in David's life. What are the tribes? Which one(s) are with David?

_____
_____
_____
_____
_____
_____

4) What is meant by the terms "the house of David" and "the house of Saul," and what is the significance of the "house of David"?

_____
_____
_____
_____
_____
_____
_____

READING 17 ~ QUESTIONS

5) Why do you suppose that Abner stayed loyal to Saul and his house for so long? How do you know whether to remain loyal to someone or a cause, when those leading are obviously not living godly lives?

_____

_____

_____

_____

_____

_____

_____

6) David asks the Lord, "Where shall I go up?" How does his open-ended question reveal David's submission to God's will?

_____

_____

_____

_____

_____

_____

_____

7) What specific conditions in Psalm 94 exist in the world today? And what truths about God and our world do you see in Psalm 94?

_____

_____

_____

_____

_____

_____

_____

8) What word picture does David use in Psalm 125 to describe those who trust in the Lord? What characteristics do mountains have, that we can have if we trust in God?

_____

_____

_____

_____

_____

_____

READING 18 ~ 2 SAMUEL 3

READING 18 ~ QUESTIONS

1) How many wives does David have at this time, according to verses 2-5? What correlation might be drawn between the phrase that the house of David grew stronger and stronger and the listing of the six sons born to David?

_____

_____

_____

_____

_____

_____

_____

2) How do you think God might have viewed David's request to restore Michal as his wife? What do you think was David's motivation?

_____

_____

_____

_____

_____

_____

3) What can you conclude about Ish-bosheth's character based on what we know of him in 2 Samuel chapters 2 and 3? In what ways is Ish-bosheth like Saul, his father, and different from Saul?

_____

_____

_____

_____

_____

4) Search for mentions of Abner to refresh your memory regarding his role in David's life up to this point. In 2 Samuel 3, what do Abner's actions and words reveal about his current feelings toward David and toward Ish-bosheth?

_____

_____

_____

_____

_____

READING 18 ~ QUESTIONS

5) Why is David's statement about God repaying the evil doer an important principle for our lives? (2 Sam. 3:39)

_____
_____
_____
_____
_____
_____
_____

6) What New Testament passages can you find which echo the assessment in Psalm 14:2-3? Given this state of mankind, what hope do we have?

_____
_____
_____
_____
_____
_____
_____

7) What do you suppose David meant when he asked the Lord for an "undivided heart" (vs 11-12)? (Psalm 86)

_____
_____
_____
_____
_____
_____

8) As David did in Psalm 86, list praises for God and list things you desire from God to help you be a person who is truly after God's Own Heart.

_____
_____
_____
_____
_____
_____

READING 19 ~ QUESTIONS

1) What was the nature of the void created in Israel when Abner died? Why was all of Israel discouraged when they heard that Abner had died?

_____

_____

_____

_____

_____

_____

2) Read Leviticus 24:17-23 and Exodus 20:13. Explain why David felt justified in avenging the deaths of Saul and Ish-bosheth under Old Testament law.

_____

_____

_____

_____

_____

_____

_____

3) Why didn't David avenge the death of Abner, as he did Saul and Ish-bosheth?

_____

_____

_____

_____

_____

_____

4) What Scripture passages can you find that speak of vengeance from God's point of view?

_____

_____

_____

_____

_____

_____

_____

5) What do you learn about the importance of, and acceptability of, acknowledging real life problems based on David's accusation to God in Psalm 10, particularly in verse 1?

_____

_____

_____

_____

_____

_____

_____

6) These days, what are some things that sinful people tell themselves about God and consequences for their actions? (Psalm 10)

_____

_____

_____

_____

_____

_____

_____

_____

7) What are some sinful behaviors that you let slide, which you should overcome to truly be a righteous person after God's Own Heart? (Psalm 10)

_____

_____

_____

_____

_____

_____

8) What overriding principle that you can apply to your life do you learn from careful reading of Psalm 142

_____

_____

_____

_____

_____

_____

_____

READING 20 ~ QUESTIONS

1) What was the source of David's power and in what ways did God exalt David's kingdom for the sake of his people Israel? (2 Samuel 5:10-12)

_____
_____
_____
_____
_____
_____
_____
_____

2) The Lord told David exactly what not to do and what to do in order to defeat the Philistines. How does David demonstrate his heart after God when battling the Philistines?

_____
_____
_____
_____
_____
_____
_____
_____
_____

3) In what ways does obedience to God demonstrative of having a heart after God's Own Heart? Under what circumstances might obedience not demonstrate having a heart after God?

_____
_____
_____
_____
_____
_____
_____
_____

4) In what ways does the Lord, or can the Lord, satisfy longing souls? (Ps 107)

_____
_____
_____
_____
_____
_____
_____

5) In Psalm 107, read consecutively versus 6, 8, 13, 15, 19, 21, 28 and 31. What does the repeated refrain of these verses demonstrate about the character of God?

_____

_____

_____

_____

_____

_____

_____

6) Look for parallels between what is described in Psalm 107 and your story. How would you briefly "tell your story"? (vs 2 NIV)

_____

_____

_____

_____

_____

_____

_____

_____

_____

7) How does Psalm 108:1-4 speak to you about early morning attitudes and activities that please God? From these verses, how do you suppose God views music and musical instruments in the life of the believer?

_____

_____

_____

_____

_____

_____

_____

8) Write down Psalm 107:1 and Psalm 108:4-5. Consider memorizing these verses.

_____

_____

_____

_____

_____

_____

_____

READING 21 ~ QUESTIONS

1) What did the mighty men's actions say about their dedication to David in 1 Chronicles 11:15-19?

_____

_____

_____

_____

_____

_____

_____

2) If David's mighty men were willing to go to such lengths to serve him, even when not directly told to do so, what does that say about the power David held in his hand over the men who followed him?

_____

_____

_____

_____

_____

_____

_____

3) Explain as best you can why David decided to pour out the water that was brought to him rather than drink it?

_____

_____

_____

_____

_____

4) How does the phrase "he poured it out to the Lord (as an offering)" (vs 18b AMP) demonstrate David's understanding of both the power that he holds in his hands and his heart after God's Own Heart?

_____

_____

_____

_____

_____

_____

READING 21 ~ QUESTIONS

5) What does this event tell you about the value and importance of godly traits and integrity in leaders?

_____

_____

_____

_____

_____

_____

6) Can you think of ungodly leaders in history who have brought tragedy into the lives of their followers?

_____

_____

_____

_____

_____

_____

7) Based on Psalm 133, what do you learn about the importance of unity among God's people? What happens when we are unified in the Lord?

_____

_____

_____

_____

_____

_____

8) What did David mean in Psalm 138:8 when he asked God to fulfill His purpose and requested, "Do not forsake the work of your hands"?

_____

_____

_____

_____

_____

_____

READING 22 ~ QUESTIONS

1) Read God's prior instructions in Exodus 25:14 and Deuteronomy 10:8. If ignorance and a careless attitude resulted in the punishment of Uzzah, what knowledge and attitudes should we be mindful of in our own relationship with God?

_____
_____
_____
_____
_____
_____

2) Uzzah had no reverence for the Ark of God. Commentary suggests this was because the Ark of the Lord had been in a distant land for so long the people lost their sense of reverence for God. How does this incident relate to people's attitudes about church and God in today's society?

_____
_____
_____
_____
_____
_____

3) What two emotions does David experience upon the death of Uzzah? Have you ever felt that way regarding something God has done?

_____
_____
_____
_____
_____

4) What's different in the method of bringing the ark to the City of David the second time? How do you suppose David got the courage to make a second attempt?

_____
_____
_____
_____
_____
_____
_____

READING 22 ~ QUESTIONS

5) What do you suppose was in Michal's heart that made her foolishly chastise David? (See 2 Sam. 3:13-16) What parallel do you see regarding openly demonstrative corporate worship today and criticism of that type of worship?

_____

_____

_____

_____

_____

_____

6) Who is worthy and who is unworthy of abiding in the Lord's tent? As a person after God's own heart, how can you possibly become "one whose walk is blameless"? (Psalm 15)

_____

_____

_____

_____

_____

_____

_____

_____

7) Which of your thoughts and behaviors might you try to ignore or pretend don't exist? In light of God's all-knowing power, what would be your best course of action regarding these hidden thoughts and behaviors? (Psalm 139:1-5)

_____

_____

_____

_____

_____

_____

8) Pray Psalm 139:23-24 and write down anything God reveals to your heart. Ask forgiveness for anything that is not pleasing to Him and rejoice in your restored relationship. Consider praying Psalm 139:23-24 regularly.

_____

_____

_____

_____

_____

READING 23 ~ 1 CHRONICLES 15

READING 23 ~ QUESTIONS

1) What changes in attitudes and actions took place between the first attempt to bring the Ark of the Covenant into Jerusalem and the completion of the task in this chapter?

_____

_____

_____

_____

_____

2) Obedience to God came after God punished Uzzah. Why does God often have to make His way clear through harsh consequences?

_____

_____

_____

_____

_____

_____

_____

3) Research to learn what was required for the Levites to consecrate themselves. What are some things we can do to demonstrate our respect and reverence for God and present ourselves before Him with a heartfelt desire for righteousness in our hearts?

_____

_____

_____

_____

_____

_____

4) Michal despised David in her heart when she saw King David leaping and dancing. For what kinds of things, especially that are not sins, do wives sometimes despise their husbands? For what reasons may wives really despise actions of their husbands at times?

_____

_____

_____

_____

_____

READING 23 ~ QUESTIONS

4) Who "ascended on high" in Psalm 68:18? Who do you think is "the anointed one" in Psalm 132:10? Who might be the king "adorned with a radiant crown" in Psalm 132:18 (NIV)? In what ways do these verses relate to David and Jesus Christ?

_____

_____

_____

_____

_____

_____

_____

6) Psalms 68 and 132 speak of Jesus. What promises has God made, which David reflects upon in these two Psalms?

_____

_____

_____

_____

_____

_____

_____

7) Read Psalm 132:13-18. Where is Zion? Do you think these words will be fulfilled literally or figuratively?

_____

_____

_____

_____

_____

_____

8) What promises of God are you yearning to see fulfilled? Write a short Psalm praising God for His promises.

_____

_____

_____

_____

_____

_____

READING 24 ~ PSALMS 105 & 106

READING 24 ~ QUESTIONS

1) Much has been written about bringing the Ark of the Covenant back into Jerusalem, including Psalm 68. What is the significance of having the Ark of the Covenant present with God's people?

_____

_____

_____

_____

_____

2) Based on Psalm 68:3, do you believe God wants you to rejoice, be happy and joyful? Is joy a choice? What can you do to create a joyful heart in yourself? What do you learn about joy from Galatians 5:22-23?

_____

_____

_____

_____

_____

_____

3) How does Ephesians 4:8-13 help you understand Psalm 68:18 and vice versa? Explain.

_____

_____

_____

_____

4) What beautiful promise do you find in Psalm 68:19? If the God of Israel himself gives strength and power to His people, and "daily bears us up," what stops you from accomplishing the things God has laid upon your heart? (Psalm 68:35)

_____

_____

_____

_____

_____

5) What acts of God need to be made "known among the nations"? What miracles and wonders has God worked in your life, which you can make known? (Psalm 105:1, Psalms 105 & 106)

_____

_____

_____

_____

_____

_____

6) Why is it important to give God due credit and declare the wonders He works in your life? What will your declaration(s) accomplish in the world? (Psalm 105)

_____

_____

_____

_____

_____

_____

7) Why do God's people "soon forget His works and don't wait for His counsel"? (Psalm 106:13)

_____

_____

_____

_____

_____

8) Psalm 106:45 shows God's grace, even though God's people defy Him continually. In what ways does Psalm 106, particularly verse 45, speak to your heart? What do you want to say to God as a result?

_____

_____

_____

_____

_____

READING 25 ~ PSALMS 24 & 96

READING 25 ~ PSALMS 24 & 96

READING 25 ~ QUESTIONS

1) How do David's Royal provision of a loaf of bread, a portion of meat, and a raisin cake to each of his subjects reflect the Lord's provisions of every good and perfect gift to his people?

_____

_____

_____

_____

_____

_____

2) Of what significance is it that all of the people said amen after the presentation of this historical Psalm related to the restoration of the Ark of the Covenant in the Tabernacle of God? (1 Chronicles 16:36)

_____

_____

_____

_____

_____

_____

3) What attributes and actions of God are mentioned in the hymn/praise song found in 1 Chronicles 16? Spend time praising God for those things which are most meaningful to you.

_____

_____

_____

_____

_____

_____

4) In Psalm 24, King David exalts the Lord. As a king himself, how do David's words in this Psalm demonstrate his heart is truly after God's own heart?

_____

_____

_____

_____

_____

_____

READING 25 ~ QUESTIONS

5) According to the New Testament, how can we have clean hands and a pure heart as referenced Psalm 24:3-4? What are some things people lift up falsely?

_____

_____

_____

_____

_____

_____

6) Compare 1 Chronicles 16:23-33 with Psalm 96. What do you discover? What do you think is the significance of what you discovered?

_____

_____

_____

_____

_____

_____

7) The directives in Psalm 96:1-3 and Psalm 96:7-10 are ways of giving thanks to and worshipping the Lord. Which of these things do you already do and which would honor the Lord for you to do more?

_____

_____

_____

_____

_____

8) The Lord is coming to judge the world in righteousness and in his faithfulness. How can we help people be ready for the Lord's second coming? (Psalm 96:10)

_____

_____

_____

_____

READING 26 ~ 2 SAMUEL 7

READING 26 ~ QUESTIONS

1) How did God accomplish a change of mind for Nathan in 2 Samuel 7:1-17? Has God ever changed your mind, and how did He accomplish this for you? What principle might God want you to learn from this event?

_____
_____
_____
_____
_____
_____

2) David wanted to build a house for the Lord, but the Lord didn't ask David to build one. What do we sometimes try to do or fix for the Lord, which He might rather us leave to His timing?

_____
_____
_____
_____
_____
_____

3) What character attributes does David demonstrate in 2 Samuel 7:18-29, and what's David's attitude toward God's promises in his prayer?

_____
_____
_____
_____
_____
_____

4) How does David demonstrate his heart is after God's Own Heart in 2 Samuel 7:18-29?

_____
_____
_____
_____
_____
_____

5) In what ways do you see the attitude toward God in today's culture as it's expressed in Psalm 2:2-3? How does Psalm 2:4 make you feel as you realize this is not a recent mindset of mankind?

_____

_____

_____

_____

_____

_____

6) What two aspects of God's character do we read of in Psalm 2:12? What actions and attitudes bring God's blessings and wrath, according to Psalm 2?

_____

_____

_____

_____

_____

_____

_____

7) What political and governing advice would you give a leader based on Psalms 2 and 33, especially with the state of our nation and our world today?

_____

_____

_____

_____

_____

8) What do you learn about hope in troubled times from Psalm 33:13-22? Which of these verses are your favorite and why?

_____

_____

_____

_____

_____

READING 27 ~ PSALM 89

READING 27 ~ QUESTIONS

1) No one is worthy of worship other than God, but who or what do people in society worship today? (ref. Psalm 89:6-8)

_____
_____
_____
_____
_____
_____
_____
_____

2) Why do you think people have little or no fear of God's punishment in today's society?

_____
_____
_____
_____
_____
_____
_____
_____
_____

3) What notable character traits of God are repeatedly expressed in Psalm 89? How can knowing this about God help you hold onto hope?

_____
_____
_____
_____
_____
_____
_____

4) How is David's understanding of God's covenant with him, as expressed in Psalm 89:3-4 and based on New Testament history, being fulfilled today?

_____
_____
_____
_____
_____
_____

5) What promises does God make to David's descendants in Psalm 89, and what are the conditions or terms of God's promises?

_____

_____

_____

_____

_____

_____

_____

6) Who are the people who will "offer themselves freely" on the day of the Lord's power in Psalm 110:3? What are some of the reasons they will they offer themselves freely?

_____

_____

_____

_____

_____

_____

7) What insights about the Lord's works do you find in Psalm 111?

_____

_____

_____

_____

_____

8) In what ways is the fear of the Lord the beginning of wisdom? (Psalm 111:10)

_____

_____

_____

_____

_____

_____

_____

READING 28 ~ 2 SAMUEL 9

READING 28 ~ QUESTIONS

1) Refer back to 2 Samuel 5:8. In light of David's past feelings, how has David's heart changed as seen in 2 Samuel 9? What do you suppose caused his heart to change?

_____

_____

_____

_____

_____

_____

_____

2) What are some of the reasons David would need to tell Mephibosheth not to be afraid? (2 Samuel 9:7)

_____

_____

_____

_____

_____

_____

_____

3) If Mephibosheth is well-provided for with the restoration of family lands and many servants (2 Samuel 9:7-12), what is the significance of David's invitation to eat at his table?

_____

_____

_____

_____

_____

_____

_____

4) David demonstrates an example of seeking to serve and do something good for Mephibosheth. What opportunities can you think of to do good for someone in need?

_____

_____

_____

_____

_____

_____

5) In what ways does David's grace toward Mephibosheth on behalf of Jonathan reflect God's grace toward us on behalf of Jesus Christ?

_____

_____

_____

_____

_____

_____

6) Which of the sinful behaviors listed in Psalm 101 convicts you most powerfully? Write out a prayer of commitment about overcoming those things.

_____

_____

_____

_____

_____

_____

7) What types of hearts, both explicitly stated and implied, are rejected in Psalm 101? What type of heart do you need to be a person after God's own heart?

_____

_____

_____

_____

_____

_____

8) What recent changes occurred in the official U.S. government position toward Israel and Jerusalem? If the standing of Jerusalem stated in Psalm 122 still applies today, how should believers respond or what should they do?

_____

_____

_____

_____

_____

_____

READING 29 ~ 1 CHRONICLES 18

READING 29 ~ QUESTIONS

1) Over what nations did David gain victory, according to 1 Chronicles 18? What phrase do you read twice in this chapter? How is it significant?

_____

_____

_____

_____

_____

_____

_____

2) What was done with the gold, silver and bronze that was taken from the defeated nations as plunder? What would a typical king do with this kind of plunder?

_____

_____

_____

_____

_____

_____

_____

_____

3) How does David's usage of the plunder further demonstrate that he is indeed a man after God's Own Heart?

_____

_____

_____

_____

_____

_____

_____

4) If David administered justice and righteousness for all his people, what do you suppose life was like for inhabitants of the countries David defeated?

_____

_____

_____

_____

_____

_____

_____

5) What does a period of trials and suffering reveal about a person's heart after God? (Psalm 22)

_____
_____
_____
_____
_____
_____
_____
_____

6) Psalm 22 is filled with Messianic prophecies. Write down the passages that are the most prophetic concerning Jesus.

_____
_____
_____
_____
_____
_____
_____
_____

7) In Psalm 60, God declares the disposition of several Nations. What nations in the world today is God likely to declare as a helmet, a scepter, a washbowl, and throw His shoe over?

_____
_____
_____
_____
_____
_____

8) How would a nation become a nation after God, and which nations might qualify as nations after God in today's world?

_____
_____
_____
_____
_____
_____
_____

READING 30 ~ 2 SAMUEL 10

READING 30 ~ PSALMS 20 & 21

READING 30 ~ PSALMS 20 & 21

READING 30 ~ QUESTIONS

1) Why do you think the princes of the Ammonites advised Hanun to assume David had dishonorable motives? What can we learn from 2 Samuel 10 about the consequences of assuming the worst in others?

_____

_____

_____

_____

_____

_____

_____

_____

2) In 2 Samuel 10:1-5, what do we learn about the importance of discerning wise counsel before we take action, and how can we determine if our counsel is wise?

_____

_____

_____

_____

_____

_____

_____

_____

3) What is revealed about King David's heart toward his men when he told them to stay at Jericho until their beards had grown back?

_____

_____

_____

_____

_____

_____

4) How are the sons of Ammon offending David, then taking up arms against David, similar to people sinning and then fighting against God?

_____

_____

_____

_____

_____

_____

_____

5) What was Joab's final statement recorded before the battle in 2 Samuel 10:7-12? What does this reveal about Joab's heart at this moment?

_____

_____

_____

_____

_____

_____

6) In what ways is Joab's directive to his brother, Abishai, in 2 Samuel 10:12 a good directive for God's people today?

_____

_____

_____

_____

_____

_____

_____

7) Prepare to pray Psalm 20:4-5 over family members, friends, church members, co-workers, etc. Who is at the top of your list? Pray for them now, using David's powerful words.

_____

_____

_____

_____

_____

_____

8) In what do you rejoice with joy and gladness that the Lord provides for you? (Psalm 21) Praise the Lord!

_____

_____

_____

_____

_____

_____

READING 31 ~ QUESTIONS

1) List the sins David committed in 2 Samuel 11.

_____
_____
_____
_____
_____
_____
_____
_____

2) How might David's position and lifestyle have "set him up" for this devastating level of sin? What might David have done differently (use your Holy Spirit-inspired imagination)?

_____
_____
_____
_____
_____
_____
_____
_____

3) Who do you believe is more responsible for David's sins: David or Satan? Why?

_____
_____
_____
_____
_____
_____

4) If you had the opportunity to confront David before he committed his sins, what would you say to encourage him to stop this course of action?

_____
_____
_____
_____
_____
_____

5) If you were God, and had done all that was done for David, how would you describe the level of anger you would feel?

_____
_____
_____
_____
_____
_____
_____
_____

6) What do Uriah's words and actions reveal about his heart and integrity?

_____
_____
_____
_____
_____
_____
_____
_____

7) David writes there is no one who does good, not even one (not even himself). What standard of behavior would be considered good by God? (Psalm 53) What can we do to become good in God's eyes?

_____
_____
_____
_____
_____
_____
_____
_____

8) For what sins should you ask God for forgiveness? List them and pray for forgiveness. (Psalm 38)

_____
_____
_____
_____
_____
_____

READING 32 ~ QUESTIONS

1) List all of the consequences and punitive actions foretold against David in 2 Samuel 12.

_____
_____
_____
_____
_____
_____
_____
_____

2) What do we learn from 2 Samuel 12:1-14 about the difference between forgiveness of sin and freedom from the consequences of our sin?

_____
_____
_____
_____
_____
_____
_____

3) In what way does sinful behavior give occasion to the enemies of the Lord to blaspheme? (2 Samuel 12:14)

_____
_____
_____
_____
_____
_____

4) How might you follow David's example in difficult circumstances, as you read in 2 Samuel 12:15-23?

_____
_____
_____
_____
_____
_____

READING 32 ~ QUESTIONS

5) What does 2 Samuel 12:24-25 convey about the nature of God's love, grace and forgiveness? Look up the meaning of the name Jedidiah, and explain how his name is appropriately given.

_____
_____
_____
_____
_____
_____

6) Why does our body waste away when we don't acknowledge our sins? (Psalm 32) How might Proverbs 3:12 and Hebrews 12:6 be a factor in our wasting away?

_____
_____
_____
_____
_____
_____
_____
_____

7) What helpful insights do you learn about sin, repentance, and forgiveness in Psalm 32? How will those with a heart after God differ from unrepentant people when they sin?

_____
_____
_____
_____
_____
_____
_____

8) What does David mean by his statement to God in Psalm 51:4? List all of the people in David's life who will be affected by his great sin.

_____
_____
_____
_____
_____
_____

READING 33 ~ 2 SAMUEL 13

READING 33 ~ QUESTIONS

1) In 2 Samuel 13, evil rises in David's household as the Lord decreed. Does this mean the Lord made Absalom and Amnon become evil? What is the more likely cause for their evil behaviors?

_____

_____

_____

_____

_____

_____

_____

2) Do you think Amnon ever really loved Tamar? Why or why not? (ref. 2 Samuel 13:2)

_____

_____

_____

_____

_____

_____

_____

_____

3) In 2 Samuel 13:15, it says Amnon hated Tamar with a very great hatred. Why do you suppose Amnon's feelings for Tamar changed so radically? (2 Samuel 13:15)

_____

_____

_____

_____

_____

_____

4) According to God's law (Deuteronomy 22:28-29), what must the rapist do for his victim who was a virgin? What additional insight does Amnon's banishment of Tamar from his house show about his character?

_____

_____

_____

_____

_____

_____

_____

READING 33 ~ QUESTIONS

5) Why do you suppose David didn't correct or punish his sons (Amnon & Absalom)? What can you deduce about David's parenting and the spiritual training of his children?

_____

_____

_____

_____

_____

_____

_____

6) In what ways are Absalom's actions both righteous and sinful in 2 Samuel 13? How do you suppose Absalom views his spiritual state as compared to how God views it?

_____

_____

_____

_____

_____

_____

_____

7) What do you think is God's attitude toward you when you feel forgotten, sorrowful and defeated? Of what are you reminded in Psalm 13, which can change your sorrow into rejoicing?

_____

_____

_____

_____

_____

_____

8) In what ways has The Lord been your strength and shield, and how has your heart trusted in Him and been helped by Him recently? (Psalm 28:7)

_____

_____

_____

_____

_____

READING 34 ~ 2 SAMUEL 14

READING 34 ~ QUESTIONS

1) If King David's heart was inclined toward Absalom, why wasn't King David willing to pardon and restore his relationship with his son?

_____

_____

_____

_____

_____

_____

_____

2) In what ways was the behavior of David's sons a reproach against him?

_____

_____

_____

_____

_____

_____

_____

3) Why do you think Joab brought the wise woman from Tekoa to speak to David, rather than speaking to David himself?

_____

_____

_____

_____

_____

_____

4) In what ways is the concocted story of the Woman of Tekoa similar to Nathan's story of the rich man taking the poor man's lamb?

_____

_____

_____

_____

_____

_____

5) What role is Absalom's appearance likely to have played in Israel's love for him? What happens when people favor good looking people over people of good character? (2 Samuel 14:25-26)

_____

_____

_____

_____

_____

_____

6) What do Absalom's actions to get Joab's attention tell you about Absalom (See 2 Samuel 14:31)? What are some righteous ways Absalom could have sought to restore his relationship with David?

_____

_____

_____

_____

_____

_____

_____

7) How is the truth you find in Psalm 4:8 a great antidote to nighttime fears and all fears?

_____

_____

_____

_____

_____

_____

8) How are the words of mankind described in Psalm 12:1-4? How are God's words described in Psalm 12:6? What instructions can you find about speaking elsewhere in the Bible?

_____

_____

_____

_____

_____

_____

_____

READING 35 ~ 2 SAMUEL 15

READING 35 ~ PSALMS 3, 70 & 71

READING 35 ~ QUESTIONS

1) 2 Samuel 15 does not tell us whether David prayed about fleeing from Absalom. Whether or not David consulted with God, what do you think the Lord would have told David in this circumstance?

_____

_____

_____

_____

_____

_____

2) How do you imagine David would have responded if someone else, who was not his favored son, attempted to take over David's kingdom? Why does David flee instead of act?

_____

_____

_____

_____

_____

_____

_____

3) Put yourself in David's place as a parent. What would you be feeling and thinking? What would your actions be if one of your children turned against you?

_____

_____

_____

_____

_____

_____

4) In what ways are David's and Absalom's plans and actions toward each other similar in 2 Samuel 15? What do you think makes them take similar approaches?

_____

_____

_____

_____

_____

_____

5) What enabled David to lie down and sleep during this desperate situation? (Psalm 3:5-6)

_____
_____
_____
_____
_____
_____
_____

6) In what way does David seem to be experiencing emotional conflict as he writes the words of Psalm 70:4 and 70:5? What emotions is David expressing in these verses?

_____
_____
_____
_____
_____
_____
_____

7) Why do people often cast off the elderly in their old age and forsake them when their strength is spent? (Psalm 71:9)

_____
_____
_____
_____
_____
_____
_____

8) Of what importance is it to remind people, including ourselves, of God's righteousness and of His righteous acts? (Psalm 71:15-16)

_____
_____
_____
_____
_____
_____
_____

READING 36 ~ PSALMS 69 & 109

READING 36 ~ QUESTIONS

1) What motive did Ziba, the servant of Mephibosheth, have in presenting David with gifts for his household, and why did David give all that belonged to Mephibosheth to Ziba?

_____

_____

_____

_____

_____

_____

_____

_____

2) What was Ahithophel's reputation with both David and Absalom? (2 Samuel 16:23) Why was Ahithophel's advice to Absalom so highly regarded?

_____

_____

_____

_____

_____

_____

_____

_____

_____

3) Summarize Ahithophel's advice to Absalom and his reasoning behind it. (2 Sam. 16:20-22)

_____

_____

_____

_____

_____

_____

_____

4) Was Shimei correct or incorrect in calling David a man of bloodshed? Explain.

_____

_____

_____

_____

_____

_____

READING 36 ~ QUESTIONS

5) Why might David think the curses of Shimei were instigated by God? Why do you think David chose to not punish Shimei?

_____
_____
_____
_____
_____
_____
_____

6) When you are weary from crying out to God, what further steps can you take to petition God for your desperate needs? (Psalm 69)

_____
_____
_____
_____
_____
_____
_____

7) As Christians, how should we pray differently for our enemies or persecutors, as compared to David's requests in Psalm 69:22-28 and Psalm 109:6-20?

_____
_____
_____
_____
_____
_____
_____

8) If you are falsely accused, wrongly attacked, or returned evil for good, as a person after God's own heart, what kinds of thoughts would you have toward your attacker and what actions would you take?

_____
_____
_____
_____
_____
_____
_____

READING 37 ~ 2 SAMUEL 17

READING 37 ~ QUESTIONS

1) What was it about David that made so many people loyal to him, who brought him food and supplies, and helped him evade Absalom?

_____
_____
_____
_____
_____
_____
_____
_____

2) What was it about Absalom that made so many Israelites turn toward him instead of remaining loyal to David?

_____
_____
_____
_____
_____
_____
_____
_____
_____

3) Knowing Absalom's character, what made Hushai's plan more appealing to Absalom than Ahithophel's plan? How did Hushai's plan ultimately save David? (2 Samuel 17:7-14)

_____
_____
_____
_____
_____
_____
_____

4) What do you think caused Ahithophel to end his life, as recorded in 2 Samuel 17:23? What lessons can we learn from his life?

_____
_____
_____
_____
_____
_____
_____

5) What truth and encouragement can you take away from recognizing that the kindness and generosity of people possibly (probably) saved David and his people?

_____

_____

_____

_____

_____

_____

6) As a person after God's Own Heart, what actions can you take to demonstrate your confidence in God when you are facing significant challenges? (Psalm 55)

_____

_____

_____

_____

_____

_____

7) What application can you find from reading Psalm 55 and seeing the progression of David's thoughts as he prays?

_____

_____

_____

_____

_____

_____

8) What important truths can we stand upon as recorded in Psalm 62:11-12? What is true and untrue for us that we read in Psalm 62:12b?

_____

_____

_____

_____

_____

_____

READING 38 ~ 2 SAMUEL 18

READING 38 ~ QUESTIONS

1) Why did Joab and 10 of his men kill Absalom, even though it was against David's direct orders? How do you feel about Joab's actions against Absalom?

_____

_____

_____

_____

_____

_____

_____

2) Given what you know about him throughout our readings, how would you describe the character attributes of Joab?

_____

_____

_____

_____

_____

_____

_____

_____

3) What thoughts occur to you about how God accomplishes His will and answers the prayers of His people after reading of the events surrounding David's deliverance from Absalom?

_____

_____

_____

_____

_____

_____

4) How might remembering God's deliverance of David increase your faith and trust in hard times?

_____

_____

_____

_____

_____

_____

_____

READING 38 ~ QUESTIONS

5) Compare David's weeping over Absalom to his mourning for Saul even though each of them tried to kill David. What is good about and what is wrong with David's level of mourning over Absalom?

_____
_____
_____
_____
_____
_____
_____

6) What does a person really need when their Spirit feels overwhelmed within them? (Psalm 143)

_____
_____
_____
_____
_____
_____
_____

7) What might you be able to do, so it will be more likely "the morning brings you word of God's unfailing love"? (Psalm 143:8)

_____
_____
_____
_____
_____
_____
_____

8) In a similar fashion to Psalm 144:12-14, write out a list of blessings saying, "may our..." asking for things you wish to see come to fruition in your life.

_____
_____
_____
_____
_____
_____
_____

READING 39 ~ 2 SAMUEL 19

READING 39 ~ QUESTIONS

1) In what ways is King David's mourning of Absalom an embarrassment and an insult to King David's people?

_____

_____

_____

_____

_____

_____

2) How is Joab's confrontation in 2 Samuel 19:1-7 different from previous confrontations of David? What are some other effective ways to confront someone who is in a superior position?

_____

_____

_____

_____

_____

_____

_____

3) David sought to be invited back as king, rather than marching in to make himself King again. What is the significance of David asking the elders of Judah to bring him back to Jerusalem?

_____

_____

_____

_____

_____

4) How is Jesus, as our Lord and savior, like David in seeking an invitation to rule in our lives?

_____

_____

_____

_____

_____

READING 39 ~ QUESTIONS

5) What is the basis for the dispute between the men of Israel and of Judah in 2 Samuel 19:40-43? What happens when similar quarrels take place in homes, the workplace, and in churches?

_____

_____

_____

_____

_____

_____

_____

6) Between Mephibosheth and Ziba, who do you think is telling the truth about Mephibosheth not following David? What makes you think that?

_____

_____

_____

_____

_____

_____

_____

7) In what do people put their hope, besides God? (Psalm 39:7)

_____

_____

_____

_____

_____

_____

8) Knowing God's great Father's heart of love for you, what is He saying through Psalm 41 to encourage you?

_____

_____

_____

_____

_____

_____

159

READING 40 ~ 2 SAMUEL 20 & 21

READING 40 ~ QUESTIONS

1) When facing a major challenge, in this case the drought, how does David determine what he should do? What can we learn from David's example?

_____

_____

_____

_____

_____

_____

_____

2) The famine occurred during David's reign; however it was caused by Saul's actions. What might this reveal in regard to God's timing, plans, and actions at any given time?

_____

_____

_____

_____

_____

_____

_____

3) From the story in 2 Samuel 21, what do we know about the Lord's heart toward the Gibeonites? What does this teach us about God's care of people who are not specifically His people?

_____

_____

_____

_____

_____

_____

_____

4) What Old Testament law and justice are being enforced as described in 2 Samuel 21:2-9? How are things enforced differently in the New Testament?

_____

_____

_____

_____

_____

_____

_____

READING 40 ~ QUESTIONS

5) What conclusions might we be able to draw about the character traits of the Gibeonites based on God bringing the drought on their behalf and their actions in this story?

_____

_____

_____

_____

_____

_____

6) In 2 Samuel 21:14, after David had made restitution to the Gibeonites, it says God was moved by prayer for the land. What do you think it would take for God to be moved by prayer for your country?

_____

_____

_____

_____

_____

_____

7) When we pray, then wait expectantly for God, what is different in our hearts from when we pray, then go on with our lives without another thought about God or our prayers? (Psalm 5) How might "waiting expectantly" impact the outcome of your prayers? (Psalm 5)

_____

_____

_____

_____

_____

_____

8) Where do you hear the voice of God? Describe what you think and feel when you sense the mighty splendor of God's holiness in your life?

_____

_____

_____

_____

_____

_____

READING 41 ~ QUESTIONS

1) Has David always kept all of the ways of the Lord? What are some of the things the Lord is looking at besides David's behavior?

_____

_____

_____

_____

_____

_____

_____

_____

2) In what ways was David blameless? What makes a person blameless before the Lord?

_____

_____

_____

_____

_____

_____

_____

3) Out of the four couplets, what is the meaning of the last line in the 2 Samuel 22:26-27 couplets? (Ask the Holy Spirit for insight) In what ways is the Lord "torturous" (ESV) or "shrewd" (NIV)?

_____

_____

_____

_____

_____

_____

4) David's song of Deliverance contains many metaphors. Which of the metaphors are most meaningful to you and why?

_____

_____

_____

_____

_____

_____

READING 41 ~ QUESTIONS

5) Compare 2 Samuel 22 with Psalm 18. What meaningful differences and similarities do you discover, if any?

_____

_____

_____

_____

_____

_____

_____

6) List the attributes of God expressed within Psalm 18.

_____

_____

_____

_____

_____

_____

7) Which of the actions described in Psalm 100 is the most natural or meaningful to you? Why?

_____

_____

_____

_____

_____

8) Write your own Psalm giving thanks to the Lord and/or praising Him. (Psalm 100)

_____

_____

_____

_____

_____

_____

_____

READING 42 ~ 2 SAMUEL 23

READING 42 ~ PSALMS 91 & 95

READING 42 ~ QUESTIONS

1) How can you ensure that you have the Lord's words on your tongue and experience what David refers to in 2 Samuel 23:2?

_____

_____

_____

_____

_____

_____

_____

2) Based on 2 Samuel 23:3b-4, describe what it's like if we treat our families righteously, with justice, and with the appropriate fear of God.

_____

_____

_____

_____

_____

_____

_____

3) What is your interpretation of the verses in 2 Samuel 23:6-7?

_____

_____

_____

_____

_____

_____

4) When has God used "mighty warriors" in your life to help you stand during tough times? For whom might you be able to be a mighty warrior right now and what can you do for that person?

_____

_____

_____

_____

_____

_____

READING 42 ~ QUESTIONS

5) David has made the Lord his Dwelling Place. What does that mean to you? How can you make the Lord your Dwelling Place? (Psalm 91:9)

_____

_____

_____

_____

_____

_____

_____

6) Based on David's expressions in Psalm 91, what attitudes and actions on your part could inspire God to protect and deliver you in times of trouble? (Psalm 91:9-16)

_____

_____

_____

_____

_____

_____

_____

7) What true characteristics of a person after God's heart can you infer from Psalm 95?

_____

_____

_____

_____

_____

_____

8) How can we keep from being people with errors in our hearts and truly know God's ways? (ref. Psalm 95:10)

_____

_____

_____

_____

_____

_____

_____

READING 43 ~ QUESTIONS

1) What were Satan's goals in moving David to take a census? What sobering truths can we infer from Satan's ability to move David, a man after God's Own Heart? (1 Chronicles 21:1)

_____

_____

_____

_____

_____

_____

_____

_____

2) Based on scriptural authority, what do you know about Satan's ability to incite us to sin? What spiritual defenses do we have available to us?

_____

_____

_____

_____

_____

_____

_____

_____

3) What was David's reason for choosing 3 days of plague as punishment? In what way does this choice show David truly knows God's heart?

_____

_____

_____

_____

_____

_____

_____

4) What is significant about David repenting, but God not responding directly to David? What might we infer about God's grace when we make a mistake? (1 Chronicles 21:8-15)

_____

_____

_____

_____

_____

_____

READING 43 ~ QUESTIONS

5) When have you been aware of divine intervention, either directly, through circumstances, or through a spokesperson? Whether you listened or not, what were the results?

_____
_____
_____
_____
_____
_____
_____

6) Why is David expressing such deep anguish in Psalm 6, without specifically repenting for his sin? What is truly causing David's deep sense of pain? (Psalm 6 & Psalm 30:7)

_____
_____
_____
_____
_____
_____
_____

7) In what kind of situation could you be or have you been to the point of making your bed swim in tears? What are some things we can do when we feel such anguish? (Psalms 6 & 30)

_____
_____
_____
_____
_____
_____

8) What are some things that move people away from their faith in God? What opens them up to the vulnerability of being moved away from God? (Psalm 30)

_____
_____
_____
_____
_____
_____

READING 44 ~ 1 CHRONICLES 22 — 23:1

READING 44 ~ QUESTIONS

1) What encouragement, instructions, and warnings does David give Solomon in 1 Chronicles 22?

_____

_____

_____

_____

_____

_____

_____

2) What is significantly absent from David's instructions to Solomon about building the temple? What wisdom can we learn about instructing younger generations from this passage?

_____

_____

_____

_____

_____

_____

_____

_____

3) Why is it important to set your heart and your soul on seeking the Lord? And how will seeking the Lord impact the outcome of activities in your life?

_____

_____

_____

_____

_____

_____

4) Why was David not chosen to build the temple, even though he had such zeal for the project? Is there truth here that we can apply to our lives? (1 Chronicles 22:2-10)

_____

_____

_____

_____

_____

_____

READING 44 ~ QUESTIONS

5) What is significant about locating the house of the Lord and the Ark of the Covenant in the land of Israel? Do you see any application for you and your walk with the Lord? (1 Chronicles 22:17-19)

_____

_____

_____

_____

_____

_____

6) What would you say is "the gate of the Lord through which the righteous may enter" in Psalm 118:19-22? How does this apply to us today?

_____

_____

_____

_____

_____

_____

_____

7) What repeating concepts do you spot in Psalm 118? (There are several.) How do these inspire you as a person after God's heart?

_____

_____

_____

_____

_____

8) How can you cultivate the qualities and instruction expressed in Psalm 131, so as not to wrestle with things you can't understand or change? How would having this ability impact your heart and mind?

_____

_____

_____

_____

_____

READING 45 ~ QUESTIONS

1) What can you determine about Adonijah's character from 1 Kings 1:5-6 and I Kings 1:49-53, and why would Adonijah be so afraid of Solomon?

_____

_____

_____

_____

_____

_____

2) Why do you suppose Nathan orchestrated the confrontation with David about his successor as he did? What might have happened if David was approached differently? (I Kings 1:11-27)

_____

_____

_____

_____

_____

_____

3) Do you think the colluding that Nathan and Bathsheba undertook to make sure Solomon became king was right or wrong in God's eyes? In what ways and why?

_____

_____

_____

_____

_____

_____

4) What parallels and differences can you see in Solomon's ride as he is being heralded as the new king when compared to Jesus's entry into Jerusalem as King of the Jews on Palm Sunday?

_____

_____

_____

_____

_____

_____

READING 45 ~ QUESTIONS

5) What did Solomon's response to Adonijah indicate about Solomon's character and about the type of leader he will be? (I Kings 1:49-53)

6) According to Psalm 37, what are some of the consequences of living wickedly?

7) What instructions or advice do you find in Psalm 37 which a person whose heart is after God would be wise to follow?

8) What does Psalm 72, written by King Solomon, reveal about his heart and his desires? What might a person after God's own heart learn from Solomon's heartfelt desires?

READING 46 ~ QUESTIONS

1) Summarize David's message to all of Israel in 1 Chronicles 28:2-10. What specifically is all of Israel told to do?

_____

_____

_____

_____

_____

_____

_____

2) What is the most important piece of instruction David gives Solomon in 1 Chronicles 28:9? Why is this instruction essential for anyone whose heart is after God's heart?

_____

_____

_____

_____

_____

_____

_____

_____

3) If God gives you a task to complete, why is it essential to remain strong and do it? (1 Chronicles 28:10) What do we need in order to be able to remain strong?

_____

_____

_____

_____

_____

_____

_____

4) What are God's primary commandments that apply to us today? Why is it critical for us to seek after and still observe God's commandments? (1 Chronicles 28:8)

_____

_____

_____

_____

_____

_____

_____

5) How can we know God the Father? And what does it look like to serve him with a whole heart and with a willing mind? (1 Chronicles 28:9)

_____
_____
_____
_____
_____
_____

6) Explain how the kingdom of David and Solomon is established forever.

_____
_____
_____
_____
_____
_____

7) List the qualities of those who fear the Lord, according to Psalm 112. What benefits can they look forward to receiving?

_____
_____
_____
_____
_____
_____

8) Pray Psalm 115:14-15 over people in your life, calling them by name. How does praying this blessing over others reflect that your heart is after God's heart?

_____
_____
_____
_____
_____
_____

READING 47 ~ QUESTIONS

1) Based on what it says in Matthew 6:21, what will it look like to give to the Lord with your whole heart if your heart is truly after God's heart?

_____
_____
_____
_____
_____
_____
_____
_____

2) Why do people often hesitate to give generously for the work of the Lord? Ask the Holy Spirit to reveal the root cause of this heart issue, if it exists in you, and pray about it.

_____
_____
_____
_____
_____
_____
_____
_____

3) What main themes in 1 Chronicles 29:9-19 do you recognize as being related to financial giving that we can apply in our lives?

_____
_____
_____
_____
_____
_____

4) What was the economic health of Israel as indicated by 1 Chronicles 29:21-22? Do you suppose right hearts with generosity toward God or financial blessings came first? Why?

_____
_____
_____
_____
_____
_____

READING 47 ~ QUESTIONS

5) Take a personal assessment. If God tries your heart, what will he find that is already righteous and what needs His transforming power? Pray to have a perfect heart for God!

_____
_____
_____
_____
_____
_____

6) What is the significance of the Royal Majesty bestowed upon Solomon by the Lord? (1 Chronicles 29:25)

_____
_____
_____
_____
_____
_____

7) What fatherly characteristics of God do you find in Psalm 103? In what ways does this Psalm help you embrace God as your compassionate father?

_____
_____
_____
_____
_____

8) According to Psalm 145:3-7, what is your responsibility to the generations that follow you? What are some things you can do to fulfill this responsibility?

_____
_____
_____
_____
_____
_____

READING 48 ~ PSALMS 65, 116 & 127

READING 48 ~ QUESTIONS

1) What is the most important point in David's general charge to Solomon found in I Kings 2:1-4? Why is this charge essential?

_____

_____

_____

_____

_____

2) Do you think David charging Solomon with Joab's and Shimei's punishments is consistent with being a man after God's own heart? What aspect of God's character does David exhibit here and what aspects are missing?

_____

_____

_____

_____

_____

_____

_____

3) Why did David charge Solomon with Joab's and Shimei's punishments rather than dealing with them himself? Was right or wrong for David to give Solomon these duties? Why?

_____

_____

_____

_____

_____

_____

4) Why is it important to recognize God as our "hope of all the ends of the earth and of the farthest seas"? (Psalm 65:5-8) How might your life be impacted if you truly believed that?

_____

_____

_____

_____

_____

_____

READING 48 ~ QUESTIONS

5) Why is the death of the Lord's Godly ones precious in His sight? (Psalm 116)

_____

_____

_____

_____

_____

_____

6) Which verse or verses in Psalm 116 form a foundation upon which you can build your life as a person after God's heart? Why did you select these particular verses?

_____

_____

_____

_____

_____

_____

7) If God gives to us, even in our sleep, and we cannot make ourselves "successful", what would be the wisest thing(s) to strive toward while living our daily lives? (Psalm 127)

_____

_____

_____

_____

_____

_____

8) How do Jesus' words in John 15:4-5 express the same truth as Psalm 127:1-2? How is Psalm 127 a fitting summation for our study of David's heart after God?

_____

_____

_____

_____

_____

_____

CONCLUSION

Do you feel closer to being a person after God's own heart than when you began this journal Bible study? I truly hope so, and I also hope you've enjoyed this inductive study of David and the Psalms.

Since this was an inductive study, it was based on your personal insights as given by the Holy Spirit. At this point, if you'd like an interpretive study of David, you might like Charles R. Swindoll's book, David A Man Of Passion And Destiny. It is an excellent choice for diving deeper into the life and mind of David.

If you're interested in other Journal Bible Studies, you can look for other titles and topics on http://journalbiblestudy.com/ ~ The Official Website for Journal Bible Studies.

ABOUT THE AUTHOR

Sandra K. Cook (a.k.a. Sandy) became a Christian when a door-to-door evangelism came to tell her about Jesus. Sandy's life changed dramatically throughout the years that followed, although those changes didn't happen overnight.

Sandy was married at 19, widowed at the age of 22, lived in poverty, was assaulted, and a victim in a bank robbery, where she had a gun held to her head. In her early adulthood, Sandy was suicidal, struggled mightily with her self-esteem, and felt her life was pointless.

At the time of her first husband's death, Sandy began to read her Bible from cover-to-cover, deeply desiring to understand the purpose of life and to learn about God. Reading the Bible set Sandy's heart on walking with the Lord. She was gripped by the love God proclaims for each one of us, because she often felt unloved and unlovable.

In her life today, Sandy focuses on godly love, above all things, and seeks to help others feel and understand God's love, and to grow their fruit of the spirit. She believes everybody is more than just somebody... Everybody is God's Beloved Child, including YOU, my dear one!

The greatest joys in Sandy's life are spending time with her husband, sons, family, and her friends. Sandy loves reading to learn, studying the Bible, photography, and singing praise songs (although, you do not want to hear her tone deaf singing!)

Sandy earned her Degree of Divinity from the Christian Leaders Institute. She is a certified Biblical Life Coach, has a Master's Degree in Instructional Design, and is a life-long learner.

Sandy prays God will richly bless YOU in your life each and every day! ♥

OTHER BOOKS BY SANDY K. COOK

WHO IS JESUS?

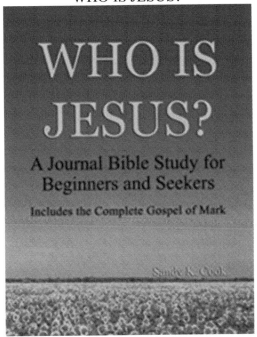

IS JESUS THE SAVIOR?

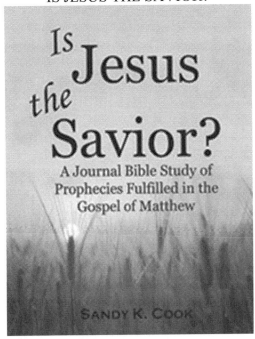

IS JESUS GOD?

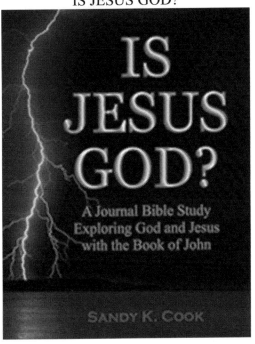

IS JESUS REAL?

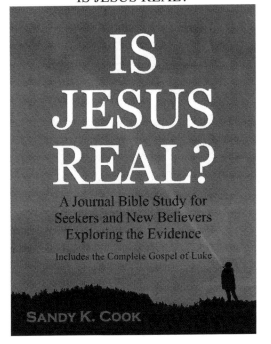

Made in the USA
Columbia, SC
06 May 2025

57617003R00113